How to Overthrow a Government

An historical and hypothetical survey of revolution, civil war, and sedition

By

RODERICK EDWARDS

Copyright © 2020

<u>rodericke.com/revolution</u>

INTRODUCTION

No matter how a government may be overthrown; the first question should be why a government should be overthrown. In the course of history many legitimate and bogus reasons have been given as to why a government was toppled.

Government Espionage

When one nation advocates the overthrow of another nation's government terms like *regime change* are employed. The designation of "regime" is supposed to convey that the target government isn't really legitimate, since a "regime" is usually thought of as an authoritarian group that is somehow imposing itself against the will of those it is governing. The instigating nation may achieve the overthrow of the target nation by way of international pressure, funding or supplying arms to rebels, fomenting uprising such as revolution or civil war, direct assassination of the leadership, or even all-out war. Nations typically engage in this behavior in an effort to change the target government to be more favorable to the instigating nation. This favorability may simply be to decrease hostility or as an attempt to gain access to the target nation's resources, transport lanes, or markets.

Revolution

Another reason for why a government may be the target of overthrow is when the government no longer abides by the people's wishes or by the rule of law such as a constitution. This kind of overthrow is usually called a revolution as it requires a revolt of a significant portion of the population. Revolutionaries are often initially depicted as traitors, insurrectionists, rebels, seditionists, or even domestic terrorists. The uprising may be instigated by outside sources or completely domestic and may be at first relatively peaceful. Many governments in an attempt to put down opposition have actually caused the uprising to spread into an eventual full-blown revolution.

Civil War

Much like a revolution, civil war is generally brought on due to discontent with the present government. One or more factions will begin to oppose the existing government and may even declare its independence from the host nation. The war may end with multiple new nations or with the overthrow of the former nation or with the complete defeat of the rebels.

Coup d'état

Perhaps the most historically common method of government upheaval is through a coup. A coup can be non-violent ("bloodless") or violent in nature and usually is an internal overthrow of the existing government without actually dismantling the form of the government. A coup is typically carried out by a military leader and his or her followers. (See: http://en.wikipedia.org/wiki/Coup_d'état)

Misinformation Campaign

Misinformation campaigns or propaganda is another method of overthrowing a government. While more successful with the advent of electronic and social media, in the past it has been used effectively with pamphleteering.

In 2016, much of the mainstream media and even the American Intelligence community were arrayed against candidate then President Donald Trump. Whether fairly or not, there was certainly a concerted effort to prevent and then discredit and remove Trump from the presidency. Trump effectively used social media to circumvent and expose the efforts.

TABLE OF CONTENTS

DEDICATIONS AND DISCLAIMERS

This book was inspired by the words of Antonin Scalia; United States Supreme Court Justice from 1986 to 2016.

> "**[The government has the right to implement income taxes] but if it reaches a certain point, perhaps you should revolt**." – In response to a question by a law student, as to what can be done if taxes become too high. (University of Tennessee College of Law April 15, 2014 - http://conservativetribune.com/scalia-revolt-over-taxes/)

WARNING:

Merely inquiring about the contents of this book or having it in your possession may be illegal in many countries and could result in imprisonment or worse. While this book is not actually advocating the overthrow of any government, its contents may be considered subversive or inciting violence even though that is expressly not the intent of this book. Please inquire about, possess and read this book with extreme caution, even within "free" countries.

CLARIFICATION:

Neither this book nor its author is advocating the overthrow of any government. The book is merely an historical account of why and how government overthrow occurs.

REFERENCES:

This book will make extensive use of public domain references such as Wikipedia.com. While some people find open-source references to be less than professional, the advantages of this approach will allow the user to easily verify sources and will allow for a sense of objectivity since an open-source reference is by nature susceptible to critique by multiple parties.

Chapter 1 History of Sedition

Most countries have laws against sedition, which loosely defined is the advocacy of government overthrow through any means besides the so-called lawful method. The lawful method depends on the governmental system. It could be through elections, hereditary succession, or some other process prescribed by the system.

The question becomes when is an act considered seditious? Does it even need to be action, or can it be words and even thoughts that can be considered so dangerous that laws are enacted to forbid them.

Since the United States is often characterized as the most tolerant and free civilization when it comes to thought and speech, having this right outlined in the first amendment; we will start our survey with that country.

U.S. Anti-Sedition Laws

The two main anti-sedition laws within the United States are:

- **1798 Alien and Sedition Acts** – actually a set of 4 bills, in part passed to quell a potential mimicking of the French Revolution within the United States. - http://en.wikipedia.org/wiki/Alien_and_Sedition_Acts

- **1940 Alien Registration Act (Smith Act)** – its main purpose was to track non-citizens especially in light of the increased amount of espionage. However, the first provision of the act addresses sedition: http://en.wikipedia.org/wiki/Smith_Act

"[conviction of anyone who]...*with intent to cause the overthrow or destruction of any such government, prints, publishes, edits, issues, circulates, sells, distributes, or publicly displays any written or printed matter advocating, advising, or teaching the duty, necessity, desirability, or propriety of overthrowing or destroying any government in the United States by force or violence, or attempts to do so; or...organizes or helps or attempts to organize any society, group, or assembly of persons who teach, advocate, or encourage the overthrow or destruction of any such government by force or violence; or becomes or is a member of, or affiliates with, any such*

*society, group, or assembly of persons, knowing
the purposes thereof."*

As you can see, even the U.S. has very
stringent anti-sedition laws. The U.S.
addressed the question of what is considered
seditious by applying what is called the *Bad
Tendency* principle, sometimes morphed into
the phrase *"clear and present danger"*. This
principle allows free speech to be restricted if it
is ruled that the speech or expression has the
sole purpose to incite or cause illegal activity.
Further, this potential activity must be a clear
and present danger. (see:
http://en.wikipedia.org/wiki/Brandenburg_v._Oh
io)

Imminent Lawless Action

The Bad Tendency principle developed through
court cases into the Imminent Lawless Action
principle. Under this principle, as ambiguous as
it remains; the speech or expression of a
person must not only incite illegal actions but
must be of imminent or have current or
immediate effect. (see:
http://law2.umkc.edu/faculty/projects/ftrials/con
law/incitement.htm)

Two examples of things supposedly not covered by the first amendment are falsely yelling *"fire"* in a crowded theater or threatening to harm the president of the United States. While the first example might be defined as inciting clear and present danger, in that potential chaos from fleeing patrons may cause injury or death; the second example is a class D felony under the law. The law reads:

> *"Whoever knowingly and willfully deposits for conveyance in the mail or for a delivery from any post office or by any letter carrier any letter, paper, writing, print, missive, or document containing any threat to take the life of, to kidnap, or to inflict bodily harm upon the President of the United States, the President-elect, the Vice President or other officer next in the order of succession to the office of President of the United States, or the Vice President-elect, or knowingly and willfully otherwise makes any such threat against the President, President-elect, Vice President or other officer next in the order of succession to the office of President, or Vice President-elect, shall be fined under this title or imprisoned not more than five years, or both."*
> http://www.gpo.gov/fdsys/pkg/USCODE-2011-title18/html/USCODE-2011-title18-partI-chap41-sec871.htm

Penalties can be applied for threatening almost any public official, not just the president and in fact those penalties are more severe for threatening a Federal judge or law enforcement officer.

JUSTIFICATION

Even though the perpetrators of government overthrow need not justify why they are doing it, they often attempt to provide some sort of reasoning. Government overthrow in reality could be for no other reason than to seize power to enjoy the benefits that come with power. However, even in the most totalitarian government the leaders will explain to the people why it is best that the leaders are in charge.

Change

But first, there must be a reason the new leaders take power. Historically, even in peaceful leadership transitions such as by election the potential new leader will advocate, he or she wants to lead because there is a need for "*change*".

For example, during the 2008 United States Presidential campaign of Barack Obama he used the slogan: *"Hope and Change"*, or more accurately *"Change we can believe in"*.

The idea is to rouse the public to the sentiment that the former government or administration maintained a disliked status quo. It doesn't matter if the status quo is statistically desirable. For example, during the eight years of the President George W. Bush's administration, unemployment remained around 4-5% and fuel prices were $1-2 less than during Obama's administration. The reasons for the statistical inferior situation during Obama's administration don't alter the fact that the *"change"* is statistically detrimental. (See: http://www.factcheck.org/2013/04/obamas-numbers-quarterly-update/)

Tyranny

Revolution, such as the American Revolution claims it had to take place to overthrow a tyrannical government. Tyranny as broadly defined is *cruel oppression.* This definition requires us to consider what is meant by *"cruel"* and *"oppression"* as both of these terms are subjective. Were the American colonists really being cruelly oppressed?

In no way am I trying to downplay the justification for the American Revolution, however comparatively; the tax burden of 2019 in the United States was far

greater on the average citizen than it was in the
1700s. There was no permanent income tax in the
U.S. until 1913 with the passage of the 16th
amendment.
http://en.wikipedia.org/wiki/Sixteenth_Amendment_to
_the_United_States_Constitution

Yet the comparatively miniscule tax burden in the
1700s culminated into the Boston Tea Party and full-
fledged revolution while Americans are presently
taxed literally even after death (inheritance tax) with
not even a shrug.

The point is, the claim of tyranny may simply be a
convenient rhetorical impetus just as the empty
slogan of "*hope and change*".

But what about when the justification for government
overthrow seems to be more obvious such as in the
government of Adolph Hitler? While modern day
critics of various government leaders like to compare
their targets to "*Nazis*" or Hitler, it is rarely accurate
since these targets have not reached anywhere near
the level of documented cruelty to fellow humans as
had the Nazis and Hitler.

How cruel or oppressive must a government be
before overthrow is justified? Is it enough that the
government ignores its own laws? Does justification
require that the government is actively killing its
citizens? Is taxation without much or any

representation enough to justify potential violent insurrection?

Perception

Despite what justification a revolutionary may think he or she has to overthrow a government, they will need to convey a perception of justification. What I mean is that there will need to be enough people supporting the cause for the cause to move forward.

There have historically been all sorts of people discontent with their government. Most of these people's displeasure will result in nothing more than grumbling to family and friends but occasionally the person may act upon their feelings.

The perceptions of the person's actions are what we are considering. Will the public see the actions as that of a lone madman? Will the public begin to sympathize with the revolutionary? At this point, the target government will make some attempt to portray the revolutionary in an unflattering light. This portrayal is supposed to stifle the simmering revolution and quell copycats. If the portrayal is not enough to do this, the government may take more hostile actions against the revolutionary, including execution. This action may feed the revolutionary fervor.

In contemporary examples; in 2014 a Nevada cattle rancher named Cliven Bundy, along with his armed supporters appeared to successfully stand against the U.S. government as the government attempted to impose actions against Bundy's use of purported federal land. http://en.wikipedia.org/wiki/Cliven_Bundy Bundy had popular support to the point that some people thought the issue might be a flashpoint for a second American revolution.

In contrast, later in 2014 a husband and wife who ironically attempted to attend the Bundy protest randomly killed two Las Vegas police officers and a citizen as they claimed to be initiating revolution. They even draped one of the dead officers in a Gadsden flag ("*Don't Tread On Me*"). This flag was often used by American revolutionaries before the formation of the United States and the creation of the modern stars and stripes flag. shorturl.at/gkwF9

Obviously, I've used the United States in discussing the history of sedition, but sedition is the cornerstone of rebellion in all countries. Monarchs feared sedition not only from the people but from generals and even family members. New monarchs would often have the entire family bloodline of the previous monarch killed just to be certain no one could claim the throne.

Chapter 2 Uprising and Revolt

Sedition is merely the overt opposing of a government. Sedition, as we saw from the previous chapter could merely be writing or saying you want the government or various members of its leadership deposed. You need not actually foment any kind of action. Beyond sedition is uprising and revolt. This happens when a large enough group acts against the government, typically in a violent manner.

Uprising and revolt can be quelled rather quickly in nations with strict gun laws or state-controlled media. An example of this is the Tiananmen Square protests that occurred in China in 1989. The government of China eventually sent over 300,000 troops into the Square to break up the student-led reform protest. Estimates of several hundred to several thousands of protesters and bystanders were killed but this effectively ended the protest. The protesters had no guns to fight back and the state-media easily spun the story so that it looked like the protesters were rioters.

Various nations of the world embargoed China and censured it in other ways, but this had little effect.

Uprising and revolt is more successful in countries where the populace has access to weapons, especially guns. This is the main reason for the

Second Amendment in the U.S. Constitution which reads:

A well regulated Militia, being necessary to the security of a free State, the right of the people to keep and bear Arms, shall not be infringed.

There is some dispute as whether the framers of the Constitution intended to secure the individual states, which at the time were not like the consolidated federalization of each state of the United States, but instead operated as independent countries (states) within a "union" of states; thus the United States of America. Or, if the right was for individual persons so that they could be secure in their rights, to the point of having the potential ability to resist if not overthrow the government if need be.

On one hand, the amendment mentions a militia which implies a group rather than individuals, and yet the phrase "right of the people" implies individuals. The original intent of the Founders is that there would be no consolidated standing professional federal military but that much like early fire brigades, a militia of the people would and could be called up for the defense of the individual state if such a time arose.

While the Second amendment debate will rage on and is outside the scope of this book, the point of reference is that before a government can easily put down an uprising or revolt, it first must disarm the citizenry. This is true whether we are talking about ancient Asia and its prohibitions against weapons, which caused the citizenry to modify farm tools into weapons (many used in modern martial arts).Or in Nazi Germany (though not many German citizens owned guns even before the prohibition), Or in the case of the Native Americans as in the Wounded Knee massacre which occurred when United States troops tried to forcibly disarm the Native Americans. Keeping the potential for armed resistance to a minimum is key to quelling uprising and revolt.

Even without guns, there have been some successful uprisings and revolts.

Civil Disobedience

Sometimes called "civil disobedience", this form of resistance or uprising and revolt typically takes a generation. Some examples of these "non-violent revolutions" might be:

1. Gandhi in India, via self-starvation.
2. The fall of the Berlin Wall (eventually East Germany).

3. South Africa Apartheid resistance by Nelson Mandela.

See more:
https://en.wikipedia.org/wiki/Nonviolent_revolution#List_of_nonviolent_revolutions_by_era

While these "revolutions" weren't completely bloodless, they did not occur through a full-on armed revolt but were typically accomplished by one person or simply an historical change in political climate.

Civil disobedience has manifested more recently in forms that disrupt the daily lives of people who are not part of the resistance rather than targeting the government directly. This is typically done by blocking roads or harassing customers at a restaurant or some other venue where people gather. This tactic is questionable since it generally angers the people being disrupted and causes them to appeal to the government to remove the protesters.

Some civil disobedience may involve defacing, destroying or looting both public and private property; especially stores. This sort of protest makes the cause look less like a cause and more just an opportunity for mayhem or theft. This sort of disobedience doesn't seem too effective since it also does not gain support from multiple types of people.

An effective civil disobedience has historically been one where multiple types or classes of people have compassion for the protesters. This generally happens when the protesters make some sort of personal sacrifice such as refusing to eat while imprisoned or peacefully congregating in a non-disruptive place and being assaulted by the authorities. If the protesters can gain sympathy from non-participants, this usually results in some sort of successful change or reform even if not full revolution.

Another way to engender sympathy and support for an uprising or revolt in this era is through media attention. Again, in authoritarian nations this may be more difficult as the media is often directly controlled by the government.

The problem with relying on media to trumpet the protesters' cause is that even if international media covers the uprising, there is no guarantee that support will be forthcoming. This seemed to be the case with Hong Kong in late 2019. Hong Kong had been a British colony in the late 1800s and remained so until 1997 when Britain returned Hong Kong to China which had historically considered Hong Kong part of its territory. This ended 156 years of British administration.

The difficulty with the handover, is that Hong Kong citizens had enjoyed a more democratic or free system of governance compared to communist China. Although the Chinese government made assurances that they would not tamp down the freedoms previously enjoyed by Hong Kong, it was inevitable that these two perspectives would clash.

China stipulated at the Sino-British Joint Declaration that Hong Kong's capitalistic system would be maintained for 50 years after the transfer. But Chinese efforts have been made to erode the freedoms in Hong Kong such as an attempt to add an article to the Basic Laws of Hong Kong that read:

"[Hong Kong] shall enact laws on its own to prohibit any act of treason, secession, sedition, subversion against the Central People's Government, or theft of state secrets, to prohibit foreign political organizations or bodies from conducting political activities in the Region, and to prohibit political organizations or bodies of the Region from establishing ties with foreign political organizations or bodies." -- https://en.wikipedia.org/wiki/Hong_Kong_Basic _Law_Article_23

This attempt caused massive uprisings in 2003 which seems to have become an annual event. In 2019, the protests have morphed into a larger cause over mainland China's attempt to push extradition laws allowing Hong Kong citizens and visitors to be subject to China's jurisdiction.

While these protests are getting international media coverage, the overall goals of the protests seem to have been quelled.

The point is, China is trying to implement the same sort of anti-sedition laws as the United States has historically passed on its citizenry, which such laws are vaguely defined.

Perhaps the reason that international media is unable to assist with the Hong Kong protesters' cause in a more substantial way, is that it would expose the illusion of "freedom" of speech and expression is thin not only in Hong Kong but in the United States.

Deplatforming and Cancel Culture

In the Internet and social media age where there should be an even greater amount of freedom of speech and expression, there has been a concerted effort to silence certain views. Often labeled "ultra-right", these views express strict reliance on the original concepts of the American Declaration of Independence, Bill of Rights, and the Constitution. These advocates greatly oppose attempts to "fundamentally transform" American culture or government into something other than the Republic it was designed to be.

Because these groups are gathering a larger following and are making advancements, those who oppose them seek to quell their success by cutting off their means to get their message out. This restriction comes in the form of "deplatforming" which is to remove access to social media platforms or by pressuring advertisers and funding arms to cut ties. This is often called "cancellation", such as cancelling television access or shows the offending person may be participating. Usually, these restrictive acts are completed by either a small vocal group or by the administrators of the social platforms themselves.

While this doesn't appear to be a direct government-initiated effort to quell a potential "uprising", it effectively is a civil war between factions; those who want to maintain the foundational concepts and those who want to move society into another direction.

Incremental Revolution

Another method to bring about change is through successive or incremental means. In this way, there is not a single immediate uprising or revolt but rather a multi-generational push. This is not like an organic change through which societies commonly evolve or devolve but rather a planned transition.

This incremental revolution is perhaps best demonstrated by the socialistic waves against America's foundational principles or individualism and free market; not just financial free market but also the free market of the exchange of ideas. The socialistic waves seek to fundamentally transform America into something else. The steps to accomplish this change are found in such documents as the book *"Rules for Radicals"* by Saul Alinsky. -- https://en.wikipedia.org/wiki/Rules_for_Radicals

1. **"Power is not only what you have but what the enemy thinks you have."**
2. **"Never go outside the expertise of your people."**
3. **"Whenever possible go outside the expertise of the enemy."**
4. **"Make the enemy live up to its own book of rules."**

5. "Ridicule is man's most potent weapon."
6. "A good tactic is one your people enjoy."
7. "A tactic that drags on too long becomes a drag."
8. "Keep the pressure on."
9. "The threat is usually more terrifying than the thing itself."
10. "The major premise for tactics is the development of operations that will maintain a constant pressure upon the opposition."
11. "If you push a negative hard and deep enough it will break through into its counterside."
12. "The price of a successful attack is a constructive alternative."
13. "Pick the target, freeze it, personalize it, and polarize it."

Of these rules, we see the incrementalism of "constant" pressure and attack. You do not give up simply because you were defeated. You do whatever you can to continue the attack and keep the pressure on and "push a negative hard and deep". There is nothing in these rules that speaks of honor or questioning one's own tactics, cause, or goal. It advocates victory at any cost.

These tactics aren't meant to cooperate with or compromise with the "enemy" but rather to "pick the target, freeze it, personalize it, and polarize it." In fact, these tactics hope and expect and utilize the "enemy's" willingness to cooperate and compromise. The tactics seek to overwhelm and terrify the enemy. The tactics seek to force the enemy into a "constructive alternative" which can be pushed even further until the ultimate goal is achieved.

Once it is determined that this is the sort of tactic that is being used, the only counterattack is to not cooperate and not compromise and instead reassert the foundational principles. It may be necessary to even completely eradicate anyone attempting to use such tactics; however, this could cause support for the protesters to increase.

Uprising and revolt typically is messy and leaves everyone sullied. In hindsight, if the revolutionaries win, they can and often do rewrite history to make themselves look more honorable and noble than they were during the actual fight. But the reality is, they more than likely had to engage in dishonorable and unsavory tactics to achieve the goal. With this in mind, the perspective revolutionary must grapple with his or her conscience. Will they be able to live with themselves after the war is won?

Whether it is seeing actual bodies strewn on the battlefield or the undeserved destruction of your enemy's reputation, will you be able to live with yourself? And if you can, should you be able? Did you become a monster to remove monsters? Do the ends really justify the means?

Historically, if enough time passes people begin to romanticize the revolution that makes it good and just. It becomes a divine sanctioned act that was destined to happen because "God" or "righteousness" or the "common welfare" of the "people" were on the side of the uprising and revolt. Anyone who opposed or continues to oppose it and its current outcome are "traitors" and "treasonous".

Just Cause

A book that is reviewing how government overthrow might work should also review why it might be done in the first place. As stated previously, revolutionaries do not need to provide justification for their revolt, it may simply be the desire for power. But eventually, historians or even descendants of the revolutionaries will come looking for the justification. Was it for a "good reason"?

Once the revolution settles and all the revisionism history is completed, it is often difficult to educate the populace about the real history. It will appear that tellers of the real history are traitors worse yet, new revolutionaries. This cannot be tolerated and will often result in further authoritarian actions by the government.

In contrast, revolutionaries may present a false history to disparage the current government. This effort will be used to justify its overthrow. Unfortunately, determining whether a cause is "just" or not is more difficult than whether it adheres to some moral precepts. The intrigue with uprising and revolt becomes even worse if it is not organic but rather is being funded by some outside party.

In retrospect, most things can be justified. A revolution is going to claim it is overthrowing tyranny or protecting itself and the country from corruption of some sort. To argue too passionately why one group of people might displace another; whether we are talking about the Europeans displacing the Native Americans or the Africans now seemingly replacing the Europeans in Europe is a pointless endeavor if the entirety of history is considered. Almost no culture or society has been unaffected by outside forces. Even the most monolithic society has incurred influence if not invasion from some other culture. We see this with Spain in the 8th century when it was dominated by Muslim rulers or England when the Saxons were displaced and absorbed by "Normands", or rather Viking's living in Normandy France.

So, idealistic concepts of an uncorrupted, "pure" society has always been a delusion. The just cause ends up being more of a "just because".

CHAPTER 3 OTHER WORDS WAR

The inherent oxymoron in the classification of a "civil war" has always been a humorous sadness to me. War is hardly ever described as civilized. We literally live on a planet where the entire population could comfortably fit into the state of Texas and yet we kill each other if we get too close or want what the other guy has. https://overpopulationisamyth.com/episode-1-overpopulation-the-making-of-a-myth/

Civil war is defined as a *"war between citizens of the same country"* – Google

Historically, civil wars break out when the ruling government attempts to impose something on either the people directly or upon a semi-sovereign region such as a state or province. This is exactly what happened during the American Civil War. When the federal government tried to force several states to change not only their position on slavery but also on their Constitutional right to secede from the "union", these states rebelled. The civil war was less about citizens fighting amongst themselves and more about the stronger, a more organized federal government trying to disallow individual states their right to self-govern. As I say this, please understand I am not advocating for slavery. The civil war was not initially about slavery so much as it was about sovereignty.

Until the American Civil War, most battlefield wars were fought as soldiers lined up on a field and each side would attempt to overwhelm the other until one retreated or surrendered and then it ended. The American Civil War was different in that it established total war, or total defeat where one side attempted to cut off supply lines, destroy cities, chase soldiers around the countryside and even employ the tactics of Guerilla warfare; where armed citizens fought soldiers. Many of these elements were present in previous wars but never so many of them in one conflict.

While civil wars initially are contained to fighting between citizens of the same country, this doesn't stop other countries from taking sides and support one or even both sides. The interests of the third-party country might be met by fomenting an arms race that it can supply or establishing a proxy nation once the winner has so enmeshed itself with the support of the outside nation that it becomes beholden to it.

A history of the most pivotal civil wars bears out that civil wars became less about fighting between citizens and more about third-party involvement.
https://www.warhistoryonline.com/history/8-civil-wars-shaped-world-m.html

It is sometimes beneficial for third-party nations to foment or encourage civil war among its neighbors. It prevents the nation engaged in civil war from becoming too powerful. It allows for the potential of arms sales from the third-party nation. It usually prevents the nation involved in civil war from uniting with other nations in the region. In this way, the third-party nation can somewhat control the nation embroiled in civil war. Understanding this may help us realize why there has been so many "civil" conflicts in the world, especially in modern times when so many nations are interdependent on others.

Cold War

A "cold war" is when conflict between the "warring" nations is either non-existent or minimal and is more about tension and competition between the nations.

Perhaps the most infamous cold war was that between the United States and the U.S.S.R. also known as Russia. The cold war began almost immediately after the end of World War 2. USA and the Soviet Union had reluctantly worked together to defeat the Nazis. USA and Russia had conflicting political and social structures that would inevitably cause tension. U.S.S.R. was socialistic and authoritarian whereas America had always been capitalistic and freedom advocating.

As the Soviet Union began to rebuild after World War 2, it began to expand its influence and territory; among which was the newly acquired eastern portion of Berlin Germany. America and its allies controlled the western portion of Berlin as per the agreement to divide the former territories of the Nazis. This geopolitical tension within Berlin is the epitome of the larger cold war tension that would exist between the U.S. and the U.S.S.R. for almost the next fifty years.

The cold war was like a chess game where the U.S. and the Soviet Union moved pieces around the globe which antagonized the other. This "game" came to a head when the Russians tried to move missiles into Cuba which is only 103 miles from Florida. While the U.S. already had missiles near Russia, this move would be the first time Russia would openly place weaponry this close to the U.S. The United States responded by blockading Cuba. As Russian ships approached the blockade, the potential for all out nuclear war increased. The situation was eventually averted when the Russians agreed to not attempt to place missiles in Cuba and remove the ones already there in exchange for the U.S. promising not to invade Cuba and to remove its missiles from Turkey which neighbors Russian territory. This encounter was pivotal in that both Russia and USA now understood they needed a "hotline" of communication between them so that future escalation could be defused.

Like civil war, cold wars on smaller scales are often fomented between nations to destabilize them. This distrust and tension prevents cooperation which may be detrimental to a third-party nation. In fact, as the colonial European powers and especially Britain began to withdraw from nations occupied as territories, the powers would often divide the nation along ethnic lines which had the effect of precluding national unity. This is evident in how India was divided into three parts; India proper, Pakistan, and Bangladesh. (See Mountbatten Plan) Pakistan and "East Bengal" were one province under the division whereas as "West Bengal" would become a state in India proper. Eventually, East Bengal fought a war against Pakistan and became independently; Bangladesh. But the point is, these tensions were caused by England dividing the region up along ethnic lines; Hindus versus Muslims. This tension still exists today. Perhaps had there been one "super" India instead of three distinct nations in the region, India would ever be more powerful than it is. So, it is often advantageous for some nations in the short and long terms to keep conflict or tensions among other nations.

Superpowers

The word superpowers may immediately invoke the idea of some person in tights and a cape but what is meant here are the nations that control most of the world's weapons and financial might. A superpower nation also may be one that is in a sort of perpetual cold war with other superpowers. This competitive cold war exists between the USA, Russia, China, and the European Union. However, after the fall of the U.S.S.R. in the 1990s, it might be argued that the USA is the sole remaining superpower and that the other nations are emerging or potential superpowers, since the USA has more influence on a global scale than many of the other nations.

Superpowers engage in activities such as space exploration and foreign aid on a larger scale than non-superpowers. They tend to involve themselves or are expected to involve themselves in conflicts around the world that really do not directly affect them.

Superpowers also become the targets of conflict in that they not only are expected to set the tone and example to other nations, they also will be criticized more aggressively for the actions they do or do not take. Their social, financial, and military decisions are scrutinized to the point where their own sovereignty becomes almost secondary. They are treated like an "international" country where their business is everyone else's business.

Not-War Wars

As the concept of war became increasingly more difficult to embrace in an international environment; since no leader wants to be seen as a "warmonger", nations began utilizing euphemisms for war. In this way, a nation can engage in war without declaring war. It has the benefit of less scrutiny and potentially allowing the head of the nation to circumvent governmental procedures that typically must be followed to declare war. Some of these not-war wars are called:

- **Police Action**
- **Operation**
- **Mission**
- **Deploying Military Advisors**
- **Campaign**
- **Effort**
- **Process**
- **Regime Change**
- **Struggle**
- **Conflict**
- **Liberation**
- **Incursion**
- **Enforcement**
- **Defense**

These alternate terms for war decrease the taboo of war, especially if a nation is engaged in perpetual wars or meddling in regions outside their scope of interest or influence.

Propaganda

Along with the rephrasing and downplaying of the scope and consequence of war is the promotion of the war to the public. This requires propaganda. Selling war to the citizens who would rather go about living their daily lives and seeing their taxes go to fixing potholes is a tricky business. It must be handled with all the finesse of the slickest marketing campaign trying to sell beauty products.

Before mass media and investigative reporting, which could counter a government's own propaganda for war, a king or a government could simply work its citizens up into a war frenzy by invoking "God" or by telling them it was their "duty to their country" to fight some other people who no doubt were being manipulated by their own government to do the same.

But once populations began to expect a relatively stable environment, governments had to gain support not only to raise the army to fight the war but to get the non-fighting population to support the war. This is especially true in a more "democratic" world where the population actually votes for leaders and laws.

This often requires the government to make a case for war by either not calling it a war as we saw from the euphemisms or by pretext.

A pretext for war or *casus belli* in Latin is some event that the government points to for the reason they had to go to war. It is almost as if they are saying, *"We didn't want to but event XYZ forced us into it."* Whether the cause is legitimate or not, it garners a cover and the government can proceed with the war. This is part of the propaganda.

Pretexts for war can be anything as obscure as saying "God wants us to take back the holy city of XYZ" to "weapons of mass destruction were found, and we need to invade before they are used". Or something more concrete like the invasion of Pearl Harbor or the planes crashing into the World Trade Center.

While propaganda has the negative connotation as being untruthful information, it is not necessarily the case. Propaganda is simply information used in a certain way to gain a reaction or a response. Is it a form of manipulation? Yes, but the presentation of any information is trying to gain a reaction or a response. Do we then say everything is propaganda? Perhaps in the Information Age, indeed everything is propaganda whether it's a commercial putting a juicy hamburger on the screen (which never looks like that when you order it), or showing limp bodies being carried away from a scene of charred buildings. These sights invoke a response from us. Certain words invoke a response from us until we become too numb from them and then the propagandists must try another tactic.

Lastly, propaganda initially was the job of the government. It had advertisement campaigns with Rosie the Riveter with her hair bundled and her sleeves rolled up and ready to work. The unforeseen consequence was that women didn't go back to being housewives after their domestic participation in the American war effort of World War 2. Undoing the effects of propaganda are as tricky as the propaganda. With so much psychological effort to get a person to "hate a foe" or join some cause, it becomes difficult to reverse the motivations.

Eventually, and especially in two-party political systems, propaganda became more the realm of political strategists. Larger events outside the control of the politician are simply used as talking points or useful tropes to further the political agenda. Everything is spun to work towards advancing the agenda even if the situation has no relevance to the agenda. There is even a phrase in American politics; "*Don't let a good crisis go to waste*". This sentiment, as vile as it sounds and is, has been an effective tool in politics and thus politicians with less scruples will use any tragedy to advance their own agenda. This includes using gun violence to push for regulating not merely gun ownership but free speech or using the idea of "climate change" to impose more taxes on corporations. The war machine of propaganda is no longer used only by governments but now by marketers and politicians and media that want to influence the recipient to take some action.

But sometimes these propagandists get caught in a falsehood or even a long-term conspiracy. You would think this would immediately destroy their credibility but oddly enough, entire news organizations that have been caught red-handed fabricating elaborate false stories, continue to "report" and people continue to listen to them and take them seriously.

CHAPTER 4 TREASON AND COUPS

Overthrow must start with either overt disobedience or with unforeseen coup; betrayal. Governments of all kinds attempt to install "loyal" people into positions of power. Whether the government is a monarchy, a parliamentary democracy, a republic, or a dictatorship, all types of governments need more than just one person to function. The leadership will attempt to install or align themselves with people with the same agendas.

Perhaps another method to overthrow a government is through infiltration. If enough disloyal people are appointed or left over from the previous administration, those people could theoretically undermine the current administration from within. This kind of behavior is considered treason.

But in the United States, treason is more specifically defined as "adhering to the enemies" of the state; typically, some foreign power.

"Treason against the United States, shall consist only in levying War against them, or in adhering to their Enemies, giving them Aid and

So, when political opponents claim treason from their counterparts, it often doesn't live up to the Constitutional definition of treason. Opposing a political party in power does not amount to treason. However, if it can be shown that infiltrators or even politicians acting in the open are doing things to bring down the current administration, we might be able to see how this destabilization could be considered "levying war" against the United States since it could potentially topple the entire government structure.

Political agitators and protesters will often be labeled as treasonous or traitors to the government or country when in reality they may only be opposed to the current administration in power.

But is it ethical to undermine an administration from within? What if the country's own intelligence agencies actively were trying to unseat a sitting leader? Could that be considered treason? Is it a form of coup? Does the person or people even care about the ethics of their actions? They are already doing something which is probably unlawful, not only within the current administration but in the country's own laws that are followed by past administrations. Usually, a country has a "lawful" method of deposing a leader; such as impeachment by vote of some majority House or parliament. But even that isn't flawless as it often can allow for a party "coup" to occur where the opposition party may use the method to simply remove the leader from the opposite party even if the leader has not really committed an impeachable offense.

Beating time

It would seem, the key to treason or coup is to accomplish your end goal before the authorities act and stop, arrest, or even kill you. If you are exposed or caught before you can fully implement your treachery, then the effort is lost. This requires extensive planning.

Since elections are often won by the incumbent, waiting for the opportunity to remove a leader from office through the ballot box may be undesirable. Treason and coup are the alternate choice and does not require voter support. If you have enough well-planted subordinates in the current administration or you have control of the legislative branch of the government, you may be able to create an impeachable offense either through false witnesses or cloture. But you must hurry while you have the momentum.

You may especially be able to make progress towards a coup if you can garner enough support by the media. If you can saturate media; including social media, late night entertainment, and comedy you will be able to craft the idea that "everyone" agrees with you even if they do not.

A coup in the Information and Internet Age isn't simply "palace intrigue" where you work to gain the loyalty of some within the administration. You must work to completely destroy your victim. Dehumanize, even show them in a light that makes them into a monster that their own mother would kill. This is what you must do if you want to accomplish a coup in this generation. If you don't have the stomach for it, or you have principles or ethics that will not allow you to go this far, then you will probably be unsuccessful in your coup.

From the inside

If you have managed to gain access to part of the government, such as being a senator or a judge you might be able to use this position to sit upon some board or to make some ruling that can help with your coup. But the key is to make it look as "non-partisan" as possible. If it looks like the political party with which you are affiliated is going after the leader, then your coup could easily be exposed. You must wait for the right opportunity to strike. If you do it too soon, you risk emboldening the leader's base and it will become even more difficult to dislodge or run the leader from office.

If you are trying to foment a coup against an otherwise successful, popular, and dynamic leader with strong support you will need tactics that eat away at all those positive attributes. It is no longer enough to design some "scandal". Voters and supporters are becoming wiser to this approach and are beginning to either become numb or forgiving of their leaders' humanness. In fact, this human side is something politicians work to present to people. Your attempt to discredit them may help solidify their humanness in their supporters' minds.

From the inside, you will need to continue an onslaught of allegations against the leader. The claims need not be true nor even successfully executed. In the populace's view, "where there is smoke there is fire". Putting the target on the defensive makes them look guilty even if they aren't.

Being a judge versus a legislator has the advantage of less oversight, more autonomy and the ability to impose immediate damage on the leader. While all of your proclamations might be reversed by a higher judicial branch, the damage and irritation to the leader is immediately successful. In most governmental systems, the judicial branch has enough separation from the executive and legislative branches to act with impunity. However, in despotic government systems a leader may just summarily have you and perhaps your head removed from your robe.

Another avenue from the inside, is within the intelligence community. Almost all governments have spies and counterspies and investigative police. Manufacturing a crime will be more difficult but if you have enough support, you will be able to create or trick an auxiliary of the leader into a criminal offense that you can use to implicate the leader. Once you have enough fabricated evidence, it is less about the crime and more about the seriousness of the charge. Internal investigations will bog the leader down enough to effectively hinder activity from the leader. You will have accomplished a sort of coup without actually removing the leader from office. Now it is just a matter of creating a shadow or alternative government until the lamed leader resigns or leaves office at the end of their term.

Failed Consequences

Through all of this, keep in mind that if you fail you could be charged with treason. If this happens, you may need to pivot to make it look like you were simply expressing your disagreement with the leadership but that you didn't actually intend to attack it or dismantle it. If you can successfully portray yourself as the victim, then you may save yourself from imprisonment and even execution. But this will require making the leader look like a "fascist"; an opponent to free speech and independence. It would even be better if you can paint them as a bigot, a racist, and phobic to whatever social class appears to be oppressed. Lay this on as thick as you can, so that any action the leadership takes against you only seems to validate your claims against it.

The best consequence of a failed coup operation will be a second chance via sympathy. If you can successfully play the victim, you may gain more support and perhaps even cause the leadership to do the very thing you were falsely accusing them. If you can pull this off, you trick history into writing your story for you and no one will be the wiser.

Obviously, the most negative consequence to your attempted coup is your own death. Historically, if a coup fails, its participants are rounded up and made to be examples. Again, even this could parlay into a win, but it will usually require someone is sacrificed as the scapegoat. The difficult part is deciding who will take the fall so that the coup can either remain hidden or allow the conspirators to escape. You can always keep trying as long as the concept remains. The players can change but the core concept must be maintained.

Sometimes, after a failed coup and the retribution for it, all future attempts die with the plotters. In more authoritarian societies, the leadership can deliver swift "justice" and so completely and brutally that no one dares try it again. This was the case with Iraqi leader, Saddam Hussein.

Retribution and Reclamation

Hussein, like many despotic leaders in the Middle East came to power through coup so he was intimately aware of how coups develop and thus how to identify and quell them. One of the first things is to create a personal "security force" which is smaller but better armed than the standing military. Hussein realized that he had to keep his domestic opponents so fearful of his retribution that they wouldn't even think about conspiring against him let alone look for coconspirators.

If a dictator clamps down too hard on the population, things could boil over into street mobs protesting and rioting. When this happens, the leader can either meet it with force or ignore it and hope it dies down. This could also be dependent on whether the mob garners outside or international attention and support. This is the reason dictators typically shut down access to their country. Just entering it without proper authorization and monitoring could mean instant death without a trial. You can typically tell a despotic nation because not only will its borders be solidified against people entering but even more so restrictive of people leaving. The freedom of movement and self-defense are the first things to suffer as a dictator comes into power. In this way, flash and street mobs are easily dispersed or even eradicated in that the mob can neither effectively defend nor flee.

Whether "Yellow Vests" protests triggered in France or the "Anti-ELAB" protests in Hong Kong, these prolonged insurrections of sorts are not as easily put down in "free" societies or when the world is watching. So, a government only has a few options:

1. **Acquiesce to some or all demands.**
2. **Wait for the movement to disband.**
3. **Create a counter-protest.**
4. **Use force anyway.**

ACQUIESCE

This may or may not work. It could embolden the protesters to demand more since it appears as weakness. The French Revolutions of the eighteenth century suffered from this course of action from the various leaders that gained power through their own coups. This course could also spark new groups to attempt coup or trigger outside forces to swoop in and take advantage of the weakness.

DISBANDMENT

This is a waiting game to see if the protesters can maintain their enthusiasm for their goals. A government could help disillusion spread in the movement by covertly cutting off the source of food and funding. It is better for the movement to dissolve naturally as any action of subterfuge against it could exacerbate it.

COUNTER-PROTEST

In example of the Yellow Vests protests in France and wider Europe, a countermovement called the "Red Scarves" formed. This counter demonstration has nowhere near the support of the Yellow Vests. A danger of creating a countermovement is that it could result in an all-out civil war.

FORCE

In Hong Kong, despite the international spotlight on the protest, the government is taking a tactical hardline even to the point of killing some of the protesters. At this point, it has not led to enough international condemnation for the Chinese government to change its course of action. If this protest had happened in mainland China, there is no doubt it would have already been put down just as was the Tiananmen Square protest in 1989.

It seems that with the instant transmission of videos and audio, not only is it becoming more difficult for local atrocities like police brutality to occur but governments; free or otherwise are less able to silence opposition. This reclamation of self-governance is spreading and will require a yet unseen solution for powers to keep their hold over the population. Perhaps the next iteration of government is a world government, so centralized that its coordination of authority is as instant as the coordination of the protesters.

CHAPTER 5 WORLD GOVERNMENT

Since this is about hypothetical situations, we should consider the possibility of a world government. Not just a collaborative United Nations institution but rather a single entity that has actual control over almost all nations on the planet Earth. Could it ever be possible?

The United Nations (UN) is an international body that was formed in 1945 to promote cooperation between the nations of the world. The formation came at the end of World War 2 to decrease the potentiality of future world wars. But this wasn't the first attempt to stabilize the world by creating an international organization.

The League of Nations (LN), which now sounds more like a secret society in some comic book was formed in 1920 after the first World War. Even though US President Woodrow Wilson is credited with helping to form the LN, the United States never joined. This, along with the LN's inability to maintain its own military to enforce its policies no doubt added to its eventual failure and replacement by the UN.

The US declined to join for 3 reasons:

1. **America's German population did not like the LN requirement that Germany pay reparations.**
2. **Americans feared joining would lead to Americans being sent to engage in European conflicts.**
3. **American women just gained the right to vote and rejected the idea of joining the LN.**

https://en.wikipedia.org/wiki/League_of_Nations#Members

WE ARE THE WORLD

There are people who would like to see the UN become a real "government of governments"; a singular authoritative body with global jurisdiction. It is easier to control one government than many. This 'cosmocracy" in theory would be able to impose its edicts upon any region and "state" in the world. It would be the true "empire" every world leader from Alexander the Great to Hitler ever dreamed.

But most people who dream of this type of situation are not marching their war elephants over mountain passes or flying stealth fighters into enemy territory to conquer their foes. Instead, these would-be totalitarians are mostly bureaucrats sitting at a desk in some international agency. This doesn't make them any less dangerous, but in fact more so. Because they usually have the policy making power to incrementally implement their ideas.

Negating Nationalism

Before the world government "suprastate" can come to power, first the sovereignty of individual nations must be eroded. The overthrow of governments need not be instant or violent or require militaries. As more nations cede their ability to make decisions for the wellbeing of their own citizens to some international organization; the easier it is to overthrow that nation without firing a shot and without a coup.

Whether knowingly or not, media often assists in the dismantling of sovereign countries when media says and promotes things like:

- **"It takes a village to raise a child."**
- **"Nationalism is jingoistic"**
- **"Nation first is isolationism."**
- **"No country should have borders."**
- **"It's racist not to allow immigrants into a nation."**

This attempt to shame nationalistic thinking comes initially from the fear that nationalism breeds leaders like Hitler or Benito Mussolini of Italy. But it seems it is now less about a single tyrannical leader coming to power and more about controlling all people everywhere. It is a type of "ultra-fascism" which ironically enough is promoted mostly by those who claim to be "anti-fascists".

When you can accuse your enemy of being the very thing you actually are, then you know you have been able to successfully turn the tables. The loose-knit activist group "Antifa" in the United States grew out of leftist anarchists. Again, ironically the tactics used by the group are the very epitome of fascism; shouting people down, blocking movement, destroying public and private property, and generally hindering the rights of other people.

Many of these groups attempting to dismantle nationalism and capitalism are actually playing into the hands of a "one world government", the very thing they fear…well, unless they control the government I suppose. The end result will not be an anarchist's cream but rather someone will take the reins of the world government and use it to advance their agenda.

So, while a world government might sound like a good way to end conflict, since all places and people would be administered the same, it will also decrease the ability to resist corruption. Currently, you can side with some other "authority" or force against whatever you think is corrupt and use that to overcome the corruption.

Quelling Rebels

Even if a world government can be imposed, there will always be people who will oppose the infringement of their independence. These people have historically been called *"rebels"*. To stop rebels, their ability to organize must be taken away. Better yet, their ability to garner support for rebellion must be diminished. This is done most effectively through public shame and fear. If all avenues of their potential rebellion can be squashed before it gains a foothold, then it makes the government's job easier.

This "public shame" can take many forms but one of the best is portraying even a hint of resistance as "radical" or "ultra" such as "ultra-right" or "ultra-left". Moderate or mild opinions and views are easier for a government to manage.

Another way to manage potential rebellion is to keep the people too busy to organize or resist. This is an ancient tactic employed even by Roman emperors which would keep the people busy attending the games in the Colosseum to think about negative things in their lives that may be the specific fault of their leaders.

So, if most people are either shamed into not being hostile toward government intrusion or kept too busy with other concerns, then the world government could advance right under everyone's noses. By the time it was completely entrenched, it would be almost impossible to remove.

Lastly, if all else fails to quell rebels, the government can simply displace them. Bring in "immigrants" at astounding numbers so that the social fabric of the nation is altered. Most immigrants are too busy adjusting to their new home to worry about opposing their new leaders. After all, if the leaders are vocal about their support for mass immigration then why should immigrants rebel?

Time keeps on slipping into the future

Fundamentally transforming sovereign nation states into vassals of a world government takes time. It cannot be accomplished in a single generation. It will require patience and coordination. Overthrowing the existing governments will require unleashing every tactic; propaganda, destabilization, protests, riots, retribution, revenge, and even execution. Opponents to the plan must be cleared out of the way.

Anyone who advocates for maintaining long standing traditions must be painted as out of touch or even worse; a bigot, a racist, a xenophobe, and whatever other terms can be applied. It won't matter if the accusation has a scintilla of truth as long as the accusation is repeated enough, it will eventually stick.

So, in your effort to overthrow the government in this manner, you must realize no setback is a loss. You simply need to keep hammering via every avenue; social media, politicians, comedy, educational institution. You have to "normalize" your covert revolution until it is the opponents of "change" that look like they are holding up "progress". Keep your eyes on the prize, which is the future you are creating through your upheaval.

Once you have removed enough sovereign nations, you can begin to implement your sweeping changes without much resistance. With most of the traditional institutions and conventions destroyed, you will be able to write history to fit your agenda.

Devil in the details

If the reader has not caught on yet, I have been purposely and facetiously acting like I am giving instructions how to overthrow governments and set up a world government. While I do believe these tactics are being used and would need to be used to accomplish that goal, I certainly am not actually advocating it, nor even desire it personally.

But I am playing the part of "*devil's advocate*" where I take the opposite position to demonstrate a point. The point in this case is that a world government would require destroying all existing governments either through armed conflict, absorption, or deterioration. Since there is no military in current existence that can destroy all other nations – short of all-out nuclear war – then that route is unlikely. What is left can be implemented simultaneously. It will require massive coordination like has never been seen before. Events will have to take place that are seemingly unrelated, but all move to the end goal. These events may occur many years, if not decades apart but are all connected. The attention to detail will need to be extreme.

If anyone looks closely and figures out the long-standing connections and begins to alert other people, then the conspirators will need to act. The revelations must be made to look like the delusions of a conspiracy theorist. Such a person will need to be portray as a nutjob. The platforms used to alert the public will need to be regulated and restricted. Counter-conspiracies, "*false flags*" and even planted stories will need to be utilized if the person cannot be eliminated through other means.

If you are embedded in the legal and judicial system, you can use that to bog the whistleblower down with litigation defense. If you control social media platforms you could ban, and shadow ban the revealer so that exposure is decreased. But even if you do not have these sorts of connections, you might be working for or at a place that does. You can use your position to influence or clandestinely cause the subversion of the revealer's efforts.

Incestuous Globalism

Now back to a less facetious tone. The world government is well on its way as more "international" organizations move toward consolidating their power and influence. It is not merely the UN but wealthy individuals and incestuous companies and committees and "boards" that often have the same players. One such consolidation was the formation of the European Union (EU) which came about fully at the turn of the 21st century. Originally, more for the purpose of a common currency and allowance of freedom of movement between countries, the EU has so exhibited its tendrils into each European country, that countries like the United Kingdom (UK) were attempting to "exit" the EU and put the matter before the citizens in a referendum. The people voted to leave the EU thus coining the term *"Brexit"* as the British exit from the EU. As of the writing of this book, Britain has been unable to implement the departure as the EU is making it difficult for fear of a mass exit by other EU states, especially if the UK is seen to prosper after unlinking from the EU.

The globalism extends itself into nations that may not want to participate. This happens when international organizations attempt to impose penalties against nations that will not comply. It is more about the "stick" than "carrot" approach, which is an analogy of motivating a horse to move either through threat or reward.

Globalism must contend with the fact that non-democratic nations are more difficult to coerce. Nations like North Korea and China have no desire to be under the rule of an international body. These nations are then painted as backwards, isolationists, or tyrannical. A military option is in play for overthrowing those governments when feasible. In the case of the stronger China, the military option is not currently possible without the potential of mutual destruction. The tactic taken in such cases is to claim to be "democratizing" those nations. Bringing "civil rights" and "human rights", and "international rights" to those people. In this way, globalism can make incursions without being seen as hostile. The target nation then can only complain about "imperialism" and "colonialism" and interference from the "West". This complaint comes off as the target nation denying "freedom" to its people.

Organic Globalism

Perhaps another way a world government could come about is after an apocalyptic event or a complete rebellion against most of the conglomerate governments of the world. After people get sick of voting for the same politicians that promise the same false promises, decade after decade and never deliver.

Perhaps the Yellow Vests in Europe and the protesters in Hong Kong, and the refugees and illegal immigrants are really just the unwitting first wave of the world-wide revolution to topple the political class.

Perhaps the "just man" is tired of waiting for Plato's "Kallipolis" to come and plans to bring it about themselves. No more kowtowing to the "Guardians". No more constant pendulum shifts of justice and injustice.

But before this organic world government forms into a stable entity, it would need to suffer plunder and defeat and resurrection; much like what happened in the French Revolution(s) of the 18th century. I say revolutions because it was not really a single revolution but multiples overthrowing previous revolutions. It required factions of revolutionaries battling to bring about their goals before France finally settled down. This is likely to be the course of a global revolution as competing ideologies attempt to dominate in the ensuing vacuum.

What emerges from the ashes will be the order of things. It is hoped that because of the nature of how it is the people bringing about this government, that it will be for the wellbeing of the people instead of the pocket-enrichment of the politicians. However, after some time, even the revolutionary eventually forgets he was an opposition to the politician and becomes the very thing he worked so hard to topple. This seems to have happened in modern USA which suffers more intense "tyrannies" from its own government than the one it revolted against to exist in the first place. The rights of the people are trampled upon by both the politician and the mob. The principles ensconced in the founding documents, those very sentiments of the revolutionaries that brought about the nation, these views are often ridiculed as outdated by the very people who swore an oath to uphold the ideas. Thus, the revolutionary's revolution is once again usurped by the bureaucrat.

Once again, the need arises to revolt. It is time to once again refresh the liberty tree.

CHAPTER 6 NECESSITY OF LOYALTY

Whether in an existing government administration or in a group of covert guerilla warfare combatants waiting for their moment to strike; all require an amount of loyalty within the ranks. Disloyalty tolerated too long will eventually turn into sedition, coup, and revolt. However, tamping down on disloyalty too stringently could cause those very things to occur.

Throughout history, loyalty has been a necessity for success, continuity, and cohesiveness. You do not assemble a team just to have it turn on you. You expect the members to be working toward the same goal even if they are not particularly faithful to the leadership.

Imagine what would have happened had Abraham Lincoln had an administration full of traitors of his vision. Imagine what would have happened had George Washington's fellows leapt from that boat on the Delaware. Imagine what would have happened had every inventor and revolutionary of history had within their ranks, those who would undermine them? Thomas Edison, Henry Ford, the Wright brothers, or Lewis Howard Latimer? Loyalty is important.

Betrayal is the worry of every leader. History's most infamous betrayal is that of Julius Caesar in 44 B.C. by his closest friend, Marcus Junius Brutus the

Younger. Brutus is depicted in William Shakespeare's play, "*The Tragedy of Julius Caesar*" and in Dante's book, "*Inferno*". Brutus' betrayal of Caesar ended in twenty-three stab wounds to Caesar and Caesar's death. The irony is that Brutus' own ancestor had overthrown the last Roman monarchy which in turn allowed the Roman Republic to be founded. Those who urged Brutus to turn against Caesar even used this fact to claim it was his destiny to betray Caesar who had been behaving more like a king than a Roman Consul in a Republic.

The now famous but wrongly attributed line Caesar uttered as his loyal friend stabbed him in the groin is:

> **"Et tu Brute?"**, which in Latin means "Also you Brutus?"

This phrase is used as a literary trope to signify when the least expected person in your circle betrays you. It is attributed to Caesar but there is no evidence he said anything while being stabbed twenty-three times. The line mainly appears in Shakespeare's play.

Departmental Death

So, while loyalty is necessary, it is historically not often achievable. This is especially true in administrations in free societies. Non-dictatorial government structures typically require many "departments" which allows for less control by the leader. These departments act almost as little governments within the government. Beyond the "branches" of government; which organically seem to be present in almost all types of governments; executive, legislative, and judicial, departments are afforded with an amount of independence. These departments can act as cracks within the loyalty "wall" around the leader. A department head may use the department's independent power to undermine the leader.

The irony is; the leader usually gets to appoint the department head. Maybe after some process of review and confirmation by another branch of the government, but the end result is that the department head should be a person the leader chose.

Again, in larger governments departments are a necessity because one person could not possibly run such a massive endeavor. But, the initial problem with loyalty comes during the transition. When a new leader takes over, he or she inherits the departments and often their previous department heads which don't necessarily resign with the previous leader.

Department heads are usually career politicians, unaffected by term limits. They typically have served in multiple administrations and through multiple political party control. This does not mean the person does not favor one party over another. An inherent bias will always exist.

Most leaders do not know enough people with the needed experience to effectively run the various departments, so they often leave the career department head in place. This can be dangerous as it exposes the leader to unknown allegiances.

A remedy to this potential betrayal is to dismiss all previous department heads and install your own. But again, most leaders do not know enough people with the needed experience. Then there is the problem of not having a fully functioning government on day one of the new administration or the delay in the confirmation process. What could happen with this approach is that the leader could appoint people who have little expertise in the department's purview and that could be an embarrassment or disaster in the future. A *fire them all and start over*" approach is not always possible.

So, another way to overthrow an incoming administration is to control the confirmation process. Hold up appointments to departments so as to hobble the plans of the government. Or, work through backchannels with the existing department heads to not only undermine the current government but to leak damaging information on it; whether true or not.

If the government begins to fail to operate smoothly, the leader may change approaches and put up less loyal people for confirmation. This in turn will allow for future betrayal. It is most likely that the new department head and the leader will come to a disagreement and the leader will be forced to fire the person. This will open the door for not only the now disgruntled department head to release damaging information on the administration but also for the media and detractors to portray the leader as unstable and weak.

Using department heads to undermine an administration is a tactic usually employed in bicameral governments. If your party can seat department heads and other "agents" or operatives within the opposition government, you can operate as almost a shadow government within the administration. Eventually, the government will be racked with the worry of "leaks" and isolate itself. It will become less trusting and appear sinister in its privacy. It will decrease access. Limit press conferences and appearances by the leader. It may disallow department heads from speaking on its behalf. All of this could then be used to depict the administration as tyrannical or dictatorial; fascist even.

To combat against this potentiality of being undermined through departments, a leader can either dissolve the departments or make sure to have enough loyal and experienced people to place in the departments before achieving the position of leader.

Dissolving the departments is not always an option as most free societies have a rigorous legislative process to dissolve departments. This is also another reason it is important to carefully consider the formation of new departments. Once a department is created, it is often difficult to dissolve and could be used against future leaders within your same party.

The Base

Politically, a "base" is the group of people that will remain loyal to the leader as he or she attempts to ascend to power and after achieving the position. The base is typically unpersuaded by opposition attacks.

If the leader cannot gain support from a solid base, with a significant amount especially in a "democratic" society with elections, then that leader will fail to win the position.

A base is mostly comprised of people that share the same ideology as the leader. This is the reason it is important for the leader to clearly define and even regurgitate to some degree, the platform to which the base aligns. If the platform is vague or contradictory, the base could abandon the leader for someone who better represents them and their ideology.

This supporter loyalty typically takes on a political party overlay. A person who supports a specific party may do so consistently because the party's overall ideology historically matches the supporters. This type of supporter may even support a leader simply because of party branding even if the person otherwise has nothing in common with the leader's views. This kind of loyalty is often taken for granted by the leader.

Political parties play on their base by what is termed as "*dog-whistling*" or sending coded messages to the base to let them know or at least think the leader will do as they wish despite other opposition. Another tactic in politics is "*gaslighting*" which is a manipulation to cause doubt. An opponent's base may be gaslit to withdraw support at a crucial moment, such as revealing some comment or act that seems at odds with the leader's stated views or character.

Chipping away at your opponent's base is a method to overthrow them. If you can convince your opponent's base to abandon him, you can prevail. You most likely will not gain support from the disenfranchised base, but at least the leader will lose support.

To create a base of your own, you will either need to tap into an existing base of people who are passionate about certain ideas or you will need to rile up or foment enthusiasm even if it comes in the form of anger or discontent.

Cobbling together a base from disparate groups takes a special talent. You could try to get these groups to support you based on some "common cause" you portray them having. The "blue collar worker class" against the "elite rich" is one example. This is easier done in caste or class-base cultures. Next, you could use race, ethnicity or even sexual practices to convince these people into a supporter bloc. But you must be careful that these groups don't have inherent disagreements that will come out later. Garnering the support of a group that opposes the death penalty while another group supports infanticide may eventually break the base.

The Independents

So-called independents are individual supporters that do not easily fit into any base. Sometimes, the difference between attaining the leadership position hinges on these people. A leader must convince these people to support him, usually not on ideological principles but on some specific momentary issue. Independents are notorious for being fickle and susceptible to gaslighting. They typically are poorly informed (Yeah, yeah. I know if you consider yourself an independent you are disagreeing with me). They have little to no principles which they will not betray. They are "cafeteria" supporters which don't usually have an overarching worldview that guides their life decisions but rather pick and choose various issues to support at the moment. You will not be able to count on their "loyalty".

The media often uses the threat of hidden or the unknown factor of the "independent" support to sway public opinion or the candidate's position. A candidate may move left or right if the media claims they must to gain the support of the "independents". If it can be shown that a large group of independents support one candidate over another, this can be used to gain further support from the independents because they aren't really independent. For all their talk of being "free-thinkers", independent supporters are often the most manipulated of all. Base supporters are usually left alone by media manipulation because the media knows they are difficult to persuade. Independents only require the correct dog-whistle or gaslight to be moved in one direction or another. Historically then, independents have voted most often for whatever candidate the media is mainly supporting.

The Opposition

The opposition is obviously any group of supporters that doesn't support your leadership. While you can attempt to garner their support, it is unlikely you will ever do so. However, you must be careful not to write them off, at least not publicly. If you gain the position of power you seek, you will need to govern even the opposition.

In the 2012 United States presidential election, candidate Mitt Romney was caught on recording telling his base that there were 47% of people that will never vote for him. His dismissal of this group was depicted as him admitting he would only be the leader of half the people. This admission helped sink his candidacy and he lost the election. -- shorturl.at/bDY37

Depending on the type of government system, there may be a necessity to "pander to" (as it is often called) the opposition. To move left or right so that at least your opposition won't be motivated to actively oppose you. While they may not like you, they may not be energized enough to do anything about it. But if you dismiss them, they may support your opponents simply out of principle.

Navigating the loyalty of your own base while picking up a few independents and yet not angering the opposition is a difficult task. It is a task that often makes principled leaders look like salesmen selling themselves to the highest bidder. Contradictions begin to seep into your speeches. Of course, none of this would be necessary if you can maintain a large enough base to surpass the opposition.

The loyalty *of* the base is often directly linked to the leader's loyalty *to* the base. If you lose your base, you may never regain it. This is the reason your opponent may do everything he can to make it look like you are waffling on the issues your base wants you to address.

Lastly, many politicians use their base during their first rise to power but once they attain the position, they begin to abandon their base. This will most likely cause the base to become discouraged and not only not support the next effort or election, but to aggressively join in the eventual overthrow of the leader.

CHAPTER 7 INEVITABLE CHANGE

Once a revolution has successfully overthrown its target, eventually the revolutionaries install themselves as the new leadership. It is inevitable that these wide-eyed purveyors of change and progress become the very thing they hated; bureaucrats administrating over the people. They become a class unto themselves. They justify that they brought about this brave new world, therefore they are entitled to some of its bounty. Or worse yet, the children of the revolutionaries eventually ascend to power and are no better than the government the revolutionaries fought against.

Refreshing the Liberty Tree

Thomas Jefferson, the third president of the United States said in 1787:

"...what country can preserve it's liberties if their rulers are not warned from time to time that their people preserve the spirit of resistance? Let them take arms. The remedy is to set

them right as to facts, pardon and pacify them. What signify a few lives lost in a century or two? The tree of liberty must be refreshed from time to time with the blood of patriots and tyrants. It is it's natural manure. " -- shorturl.at/oHJO2

The Liberty Tree was an elm tree in Boston around which American revolutionaries would gather for protests against the British. This site is not only important as the precursor to the eventual American Revolution but for the better understanding of Jefferson's comments. Jefferson, even though part of the government in 1787, realized that someday it would be necessary to once again "refresh the Liberty Tree" by reminding those in power that the people will resist and defy the government, with arms if necessary if and when it infringes upon their rights. Jefferson even admits that some lives may need to be lost to remind the government of the people's rights.

Such a comment in the present USA would be grounds for treason, sedition, and insurrection charges. Clearly, Jefferson himself would be in prison.

But this idea of the inevitability of change isn't unique to Jefferson. The Greeks spoke of this cycle as the

Kyklos; the natural political and governmental cycle of change. Of degradation and reform, apathy, degradation and reformation again.

While the cycle may have different "spokes" depending on which version of the Kyklos or Tytler's Circle you view, it typically goes something like this:

"…the three basic forms of government, [are] democracy, aristocracy, and monarchy and the three degenerate forms of each of these governments ochlocracy, oligarchy, and tyranny. Originally society is in ochlocracy but the strongest figure emerges and sets up a monarchy. The monarch's descendants, who because of their family's power lack virtue, become despots and the monarchy degenerates into a tyranny. Because of the excesses of the ruler the tyranny is overthrown by the leading citizens of the state who set up an aristocracy. They too quickly forget about virtue and the state becomes

an oligarchy. These oligarchs are overthrown by the people who set up a democracy. Democracy soon becomes corrupt and degenerates into ochlocracy, beginning the cycle anew." – https://en.wikipedia.org/wiki/Kyklos

Sometimes, democracy is added to the degenerate portion of cycle because democracies are more or less government by mob rule. In democracies, the rights of the individual suffer at the hands of a vocal majority even it not a numerical majority.

This cycle or circle of government has been addressed by everyone from Plato to Niccolo Machiavelli. It is then naive to believe your "rule" or "realm" (Reich) as the Nazis called their dominance will be forever, or even a thousand years. Most free societies limit the length of time a leader may preside over the government. This is typically in limited terms, with each term being between two and six years. This limited term system seems to pacify would be revolutionaries enough that they do not usually attempt to overthrow the entire government but rather wait their "turn" at presiding over it. This creates a bicameral political system where there are typically two main parties even if there are lesser parties. This constant tension of "us against them" seems to satisfy the innate and inevitable human need to "refresh the liberty tree" every two to six years.

Yet, at some point the people will grow weary of the constant back and forth of electoral systems. They will see through the "I-can't-do-anything-without-the-support-of-the-other-party" excuses that politicians give for not keeping their campaign promises. It is at this point that the voter stops voting for the lesser of the two evils and begins to see all of it as evil and needing drained like some cesspool swamp. The slogans of "hope and change" no longer suffice. The people require radical action. They look for leadership that will stop playing the same-horse-different-rider game. They will no longer be anyone's loyal base. At this point, a leader can step into the fray and if dynamic enough can take the people into a new direction.

These moments in history have been punctuated with leaders that truly revolutionize their countries. The outcome is not always positive. While Hitler initially improved the situation for Germany, it eventually became a liability and a corruption too much to bear. Nazi Germany would not be allowed to exist even with Hitler out of the picture. Other leaders have had a positive and lasting influence, not only on their own countries but on the world.

One example might be Franklin Delano Roosevelt (FDR), thirty-second president of the United States.

His administration was the longest lasting in the U.S. and before the mandatory term limits. During his four terms as president, FDR was able to pass many of the social compacts found in his "New Deal" political philosophy; such as social security. This was partly due to the fact that the people, the voters were in crisis over the "Great Depression" which engulfed much of the world economies at the time. FDR became that leadership that emerged from the chaos. He was able to push through programs the people otherwise might oppose since those programs would eventually infringe upon personal liberty.

It was during FDR's presidency that the terms "liberal" and "conservative" gained their present meaning. A liberal was someone that favored FDR's socialistic programs. A conservative was someone who wanted to maintain the individual liberties encapsulated in the foundation of the USA. This tension continued to exist for many decades after FDR and has been the pretext for rallying the base of either side. However, it appears the American electorate is almost at the point where they see little difference between liberals and conservatives. A real revolution may be on the horizon.

Unless some sort of leadership presents itself that can generate a sustained base of loyal supporters, it seems that the USA may soon experience its own Kyklos cycle or Liberty Tree refreshing. It will require a leader that distinguishes him or herself as different than both parties. Someone loyal to the individual. If not, the resultant power vacuum could lead to an armed revolution or civil war. Perhaps this change is inevitable.

Power Vacuum

If the perspective leader cannot generate enough base support by cobbling together disparate groups, he or she could wait for or create a power void or vacuum. This vacuum could simply be an untapped political niche or the complete breakdown in voter trust of the entire political system. Either way, this vacuum will allow the leader an advantage over the candidates that continue to play the same political game.

Exposing and using this scenario is a type of government overthrow. It allows the perspective leader the ability to marshal agents and activists for his or her cause without the people even realizing they are being used in this manner. The leader's detractors may see this and claim it is "cultish" since they themselves cannot muster the same kind of devotion. Such a dynamic leader can almost do no wrong in the eyes of his supporters. This can be detrimental even to a benevolent leader in that it could cause him to act too arrogantly. While his ego or confidence would not necessarily be wrong, it may cause him to not realize vulnerabilities around him.

Multiple, potential leaders vying within a power vacuum has historically been brutal. This typically happens after the fall of a monarchy; the children of the monarch then fight over the throne. Because of this possibility, monarchs would often give their children minor "kingdoms" or regions to rule, hoping they would be satisfied, especially since many children of kings and queens would not wait until their parents died before trying to take their crown.

Killing your father (the king) is called "patricide" or "regicide" if he's a "regent" (ruler). While this is certainly one way to overthrow a government, it is not as acceptable in "free" countries and most likely will get you arrested or executed.

Change you can believe in

No matter how well the previous administration governed, you will need to depict them as flawed or incompetent. You will need to convince the people that you are bringing "change" and "progress" that will make everything better. You can do this through slogans that say as much and through talking down the successes of the administration you are trying to oust. The danger of doing this is that it could have such negative repercussions that it actually does depress the economy and the people's outlook on the country. If you generate a toxic atmosphere, you might end up inheriting it when you do gain power. So, while you may have manufactured your opponent's failures, yours may be real.

Obviously, the most ethical and "moral" thing to do is to really provide a positive change. But all change is not positive. You will need to decide if the change you plan to bring is actually going to benefit the people or if you're just feeding them bullshit to gain their trust. And if you are providing fake hope and change, can you live with yourself?

Fortunately for you, living in the Information Age affords you the ability to market yourself like never before. You can print out glossy photos of yourself kissing babies and holding umbrellas over little old ladies in the rain. You can twist your opponent's history into showing a "bigot" or a "racist" even if it isn't factual. If you say it long enough and get enough of the right people to repeat the claim, then you can win.

Perhaps you don't want to go this route. Maybe you want to go high when your opponents go low. You might want to send a more "civil" tone or message. Unfortunately, no matter how much the public claims it doesn't want to see political fights, these fights are what sway supporters one way or another. Moderate, mild politicians rarely generate enough support to gain power. It takes someone with gumption and grit to come out on top. Feckless handwringers seem to be relegated to supporting roles or multi-time losing streaks no matter how "qualified" they or their supporters think they are.

But if you do gain power and with enough dominance, you might be able to cause real change. Controlling multiple branches of government should be a goal. If all you become is the executive or military leader of your country, your dictates are easily undone by the next occupant of that office. You will need legislative and judicial allies that will not only help you completely implement your changes but also maintain and safeguard those changes even when you are no longer in power.

So many leaders seek a "legacy", a footprint of their time in the big chair. They will work their entire tenure to carefully craft this legacy just to see it all destroyed by the next leader. It is important that you look at the long-term goal that allies with partners of your legacy. The legacy will need to be ideological not individual.

The changes you implement will need to contain ramifications that will trigger if anyone attempts to undo them. Having policies or programs named after you will not be enough to shield it from dissolution.

However, if your changes are so far removed from your name, people in the future will not equate it with you. Social Security Insurance is not called the FDR Retirement Program…or the FDR Retirement Scam if you are a detractor. Very few changes that people will eventually take for granted are still associated with the leader that initiated and completed the change.

So, the change you seek may be inevitable, but it is not eternal. Someone or something will eventually come along and change your "change". They will seek to fundamentally transform entire structures no matter how well grounded and tested. They seem to want to change for change's sake and they can rally enough people with their slogans to do it often enough.

I'm sure when Hitler rose to power, he dreamed of his name being uttered for centuries as the man who saved Germany and united Europe. Overthrowing governments may not be as pleasing to the ego as one may assume. Your visions of throngs of school children lining streets to get a glimpse of your image as you pass by in your motorcade could as easily end by a shot from a book repository or a grassy knoll.

Whether you overthrow a government via armed conflict or hanging ballot chads, you may be disappointed with the outcome. Make sure it is worth it.

CHAPTER 8 NATION BUILDING

Nation building was a term in vogue during U.S. President George Herbert Walker Bush's term in office in the years 1989-1993. Bush was a long time State Department/CIA operative before becoming president, so he was accustomed to the idea that the USA needed to guide nations into the direction these departments wanted. The State Department and CIA like many departments often imagine themselves as independent from the current Commander in Chief.

Nation building or State building as Bush and people like him supposed; is the act of intervening in the development of a nation so that its direction ultimately benefits a specific agenda. This agenda need not necessarily be beneficial to the United States, as much of the agenda of the State Department and CIA is at odds with the long-term benefit of USA.

Traditionally, nation building occurs once the target nation has been defeated either via war or some sort of collapse such as economic breakdown through sanctions or tariffs. This is what happened after World War 2 when the U.S. and the Allies performed "nation building" on the militarily defeated Germany, Italy, and Japan otherwise known as the Axis Powers.

Being Proud

One of the key components of nation building is instilling a new national pride. To do this, the Allies had to first remove the previous national pride of Germany and Japan. National pride may be linked to a shared ideology such as Nazism in Germany and Shintoism in Japan. The U.S. effectively outlawed these ideologies in both countries.

This allowed the U.S. to restructure the nations and their constitutions around a more "democratic" format. Replacing the almost demigod worship of the nation's leaders with a more secular mindset helps to ensure that those nations will not return to their former hostilities.

In the case of Germany, Hitler behaved like a "father" to the entire nation. The people became psychologically and emotionally devoted to this "parent" and thus would do almost anything he commanded.

In the case of Japan, Shintoism was an eight-century ancestor-worship religion with the emperor of Japan being the god-like ancestor to which everyone submitted.

 The Allies effectively rewrote the constitutions of both Germany and Japan to erase these ideologies from public life. Shintoism was removed from government and left as a personal expression.

This is a form of government overthrow by deconstructing the heart of the government without destroying the people. It is not completely of form of colonialism or imperialism as the "rebuilt" nation is given an amount of autonomy once it is seen to be working toward the agenda that the nation building process intends.

During two other nation building experiments, the architects did not follow the pattern established in the successful nation building of Germany and Japan.

The defeat of Afghanistan and Iraq in the years 2001 and 2003 respectively, the U.S. eventually assisted in rewriting the constitutions of those nations. But this time, instead of stripping the aggressive ideology from the State, Islam was allowed to dominate and permeate so that true freedom is not possible.

Besides the Preambles which are replete with adoring referencing to Allah (not a generic "god" deity), the Articles within those constitutions make it impossible for freethinking.

No law shall contravene the tenets and provisions of the holy religion of Islam in Afghanistan. – Article 3 of the Afghanistan Constitution

Article 2A of the Iraqi Constitution is similar.

No law may be enacted that contradicts the established provisions of Islam.

However, this contradicts Article 2 paragraph 2 which reads:

This Constitution guarantees the Islamic identity of the majority of the Iraqi people and guarantees the full religious rights to freedom of religious belief and practice of all individuals such as Christians, Yazidis, and Mandean Sabeans.

How can a person freely practice their religious belief if the laws of the nation may be completely at odds with their religion because those laws are in line with a competing religion?

Whomever in the U.S. allowed Afghanistan and Iraq to perpetuate the very ideology that gave rise to and cause of those nation's overthrow clearly knows little about history.

Mind Games Forever

This ideology eradication is more surreptitious than mere propaganda. It is not dropping leaflets from ten thousand feet. It doesn't even require military conflict. All it requires is a constant barrage upon your opponent; whether an individual leader or the people of a nation. It is convincing the opponent, or at least enough people that what is happening is organic and not at all fueled by outside forces. It is a type of covert spy craft that has been honed not only by intelligence agencies around the globe but by media and politicians. This is what happened in the "Arab world" in the early 2010s. This campaign against mainly Muslim countries was labelled the "Arab Spring". This consisted of protests and armed uprising by people who believed they were acting independently to overthrow the "oppressive regimes" that often had governed their countries for decades.

In this way, we bypass the direct military action and the need for the overt ideological changes. The destabilization of the nation is enough to allow opportunity for nation building. But this is risky because mobs are unpredictable and difficult to control. If they perceive you are trying to control them, you may become the new target. So, with the Arab Spring there had to be just enough social media stoking to initiate the uprisings and then sit back and allow it to take course.

"**The effects of the Tunisian Revolution spread strongly to five other countries: Libya, Egypt, Yemen, Syria and Bahrain, where either the regime was toppled or major uprisings and social violence occurred, including riots, civil wars or insurgencies. Sustained street demonstrations took place in Morocco, Iraq, Algeria, Iranian Khuzestan, Lebanon, Jordan, Kuwait, Oman and Sudan. Minor protests occurred in Djibouti, Mauritania, the Palestinian National Authority, Saudi Arabia, and the Moroccan-occupied Western Sahara.**" –
https://en.wikipedia.org/wiki/Arab_Spring

The intent was to remove as many of the old guard leaders of these nations as possible so as to allow handpicked successors. This is most evident in how U.S. President Barack Obama appeared to install Mohamed Morsi after the Egyptian Civil War of 2011 but abandoned Morsi in 2013 when a subsequent revolt ousted Morsi. shorturl.at/acxG6

This nation building utilizing the cover of the Arab Spring extends into much of Obama's two terms in office and appears to be responsible for the overthrow of multiple nations including Tunisia, Egypt, Libya, and Yemen among others.

Where this strategy failed was in Syria. By the time the revolts made their way to Syria, it appears the president of Syria (supported by Russia) dug in and was not going to step aside and be dragged out to the street, and sodomized with and then stabbed to death by bayonets like Libyan leader Muammar Gaddafi.

It seems to be the perfect disguise to have a U.S. president that was so often accused of being a Muslim or an Islamic sympathizer be the one that helped to remove governments in mainly Islamic nations.

The New Propaganda Machine

Facebook, Twitter, Reddit and other social media platforms have become tools that not only the governments of the world but various organizations with an agenda can tap into to sway and influence public opinion. In fact, on the social media platform called Instagram, there are a host of people called "influencers" who daily attempt to persuade their followers to buy a product or perform an activity.

Whereas during the age of air warfare, it was common to drop thousands of leaflets on the enemy population in attempt to get the civilians and soldiers to revolt, this new propaganda machine drops its virtual leaflets into the faces of every user that scrolls by it on their electronic devices. They are targeted and manipulated even more stealthily than a well-placed hamburger commercial showing a juicy patty sitting beside a frosty drink with condensation dripping down the side of the cup. The new propaganda machine is hyper marketing techniques.

Nation building is now available to more than just governments. Anyone with large amounts of money or influence can attempt to direct public opinion through social media platform. But again, it must be done secretively enough that those being duped do not realize they are being manipulated.

The key is to target and saturate the information the would-be rioters are getting. If you can get mainstream media to repeat the propaganda and make it "go viral" as is the term in mass media campaigns, then you will be able to push your agenda.

Where this tactic seemed to fail was in the 2016 U.S. Presidential election. The media, late night talk show hosts, comedians, much of the upper echelons of the American intelligence agencies, along with the other candidates were arrayed against candidate Donald Trump. His mere entrance into the race for president was viewed as a joke and lampooned mercilessly. Many thought his campaign was a marketing stunt for his brand; that he'd drop out somewhere along the way.

Obama was certain that his handpicked successor; which oddly enough was not his Vice President which is traditional would easily sail into the office. He even said of Hillary Clinton:

> **"There has never been a man or a woman, not me, not Bill [Clinton], nobody more qualified than Hillary Clinton to serve as president of the United States of America"** --
> shorturl.at/chmE0

Neither this glowing endorsement, nor the rigging of the Democratic Party primary, nor the onslaught of sarcastic attacks against Trump could propel Clinton to the office. Somehow, Trump had outsmarted even the most expert pollsters and political pundits that assumed they could not only influence but predict and maybe pick the next leader of the USA in a sort of nation building of their own.

Trump was able to connect and become "relatable" to the general public; the people who still thought of America as that bastion of individuality over groups and classes of people constantly fighting for "rights" real or imagined.

So, after Trump was inaugurated as the forty-fifth president of the United States of America, if not before the real campaign against him began. The powers that be failed to see him as a serious and viable threat to their own bipartisan dance every election and by not recognizing and dismissing him, Trump was able to beat them at their own game. He is like a rookie football quarterback that comes onto the field out of nowhere and shows up the long-standing champions that were groomed for the position. Trump wasn't supposed to happen. The people weren't actually supposed to have a say in the election without being conditioned by the propaganda machine.

This part of the book isn't a "pro-Trump" screed but rather is trying to show how overthrowing a government can be accomplished in many ways. While even his enemies disdain Trump, they admire his connection with the electorate and often try to duplicate it.

To bring down Trump, his opponents have accused him of election fraud with the help of the Russians, yet even after manufacturing false evidence and using the FISA courts and the FBI and conducting a multi-year "investigation" ran by a political hack they termed a "special prosecutor" they were not able to make it stick.

When this effort failed, the so-called "deep state" which is comprised of career politicians and intelligence operatives launched an all-out effort to impeach Trump. However, the U.S. Constitution is clear that:

"**The President, Vice President and all civil Officers of the United States, shall be removed from Office on Impeachment for, and Conviction of, Treason, Bribery, or other high Crimes and Misdemeanors.**" – Article 2 Section 4

It is the definition of the four "crimes" that is in question whenever these charges are brought against a sitting president. The idea that the president flouted public trust seems to be enough for impeachment yet who gets to say what is public trust?

At the time of this writing, Trump was merely impeached but not removed from office, which requires a trial in the Senate.

The point is, you can overthrow a government via armed conflict, through an election process, or even through a legislative coup that is based on a very vague interpretation of existing laws. And now in the marketing and information age, you can do so from the comfort of your posh multi-million-dollar estate or from your ratty neighborhood with a few masked friends and a box full of Molotov cocktails. It's an open-source world of revolution and civil war that allows almost anyone to play the game.

CHAPTER 9 UTOPIA

At the end of the day, the revolutionary thinks he or she is either bringing a better world to the people or the revolutionary simply wants power over the people. Either way, it is a type of Utopia building for the people or those in charge.

But what will this Utopia look like? Will it be a despot's dream like the U.S. soldiers found in Iraq after the fall of Saddam Hussein? He had many residences with pristine pools and soft couches sitting under chandeliers gilded with gold and silver while many Iraqis lived in hovels. Or will this Utopia be dull and gray with everyone having all things in common like China's revolution under Mao Zedong in 1949?

Human nature is to be free; I mean free from imposition by others. Most of us simply want to be left alone and live our lives out quietly. We neither want people telling us what we can and can't do, nor us telling them. But in a civilization, there must be order. The questions are; who gets to decide what is order and who has the authority or power to enforce their ideas of order? Revolutions and civil wars often pivot on these questions. The revolutionary believes they have a better idea, or they do not recognize or submit to the authority or power of the current "order-imposer". Can it ever then be achieved that there is real Utopia in the world with no more wars? Won't someone always think they deserve to be in charge or have more resources or more chandeliers hanging over couches?

Politicians and gun-toting usurpers promise they can bring about peace if just given the chance; if people just follow, if people just submit, if people just help eradicate those who won't follow or won't submit.

One of the main reasons Utopia or paradise on earth will never be possible is because people have different definitions of it. Or further yet, people don't want it. Some of us want to struggle, but struggle in our own way. It makes us feel alive. Living in a perfect world where everything you want and need is provided would be a boring and dead world. Yes, we may have trials, but they are our trials.

Many people look to international organizations like the United Nations to bring about this Utopia. Politicians of sovereign countries often promise their citizens if they cede their independence, they will live in this Utopia imposed and maintained by white helmeted men. But isn't that really naïve to suppose the leaders at the U.N. are more concerned about your welfare than some local politician whom you can at least somewhat hold accountable?

If we can ever actually achieve anything like a coexisting, peaceful world it will require not a legislative or military-boot peace but rather a voluntary peace, where the people accept it without imposition. But who will do that? Can we trust other people enough to manage this Utopia? Or maybe since we are in the electronic age, there would be no individual leaders and instead all decisions are based on majority vote of all citizens and the facilitators simply implement the decision without question. Is this kind of true "democracy" even a good idea? Who says the majority is always going to come to a good decision? What about the rights of the individual in such a democracy? This mob rule potentiality is why America's founders decidedly opposed democracies; they always devolve into mob rule and the rights of individual being infringed upon for the "good of the people".

Republican versus Democratic Utopia

We are not talking about political parties but rather we mean forms of government. A Republic is supposed to be based on a shared contract such as a constitution that protects the rights of the individual over the wishes of the government and the mob. Think about how many laws protect individuals over the wanton seizure of their property. Today, the distinction between a Republic and Democracy is not often made and even if acknowledged, is muddled with protestations that they are basically the same thing. The person making that argument usually is advocating for a democratic form of government. A utopia could never be democratic.

Plato, the Greek philosopher who wrote the hypothetical state-craft book called *The Republic*, envisioned the citizenry dictating to the Guardians their political desires, wherein the Guardians would carry out the citizens' wishes. What Plato seemed to fail to account is that the citizenry could be corrupt and yet in his scheme, the Guardians would have to still do as they say. Eventually, all "democracies" will reach this level of corruption because humans by nature are self-serving. This self-serving nature keeps us from giving away everything we have and dying of starvation or lack of proper shelter. But people may consider their own basic survival to include more luxuries than other people. They will eventually need to take away other people's sustenance to maintain their own version of existence. The Utopia is then shattered.

To maintain the envisioned utopia, the revolutionary may need to implement a "for the good of the people" policy which includes hostility towards, if not all out extermination of the people who will not comply with the policy. This has been the course of action with revolutionaries turned "statesmen" like Cuba's Fidel Castro or Ernesto "Che" Guevara; the revolutionaries of South, Central America and the Caribbean.

The "reforms" of revolutionaries often include "tribunals", firing squads and other methods to purge disobedience and enemy "collaborators". Once this process is complete, then is supposed to come, the Utopia promised by the revolution.

Try, Try again

The typical problem with promises of Utopia is that the process has been tried many times before in history; whether a socialistic dream state or a kingdom with a noble monarch on the throne, these governments always fail to deliver the paradise described in the brochure. Usually, only the party-loyalists enjoy the benefits of the "people's" sacrifices.

So, if you are a revolutionary and you envision that you can do it right this time, you will be up against millennia of failure. You will not be able to control every element of how your revolution takes place or how it is received or developed after its success. It's possible you won't even live to see it implemented.

However, trial and error are the hallmarks of success, whether in business or nation building. The revolution that brought about the United States of America and its founding principles and documents were predicated on studying the trials and errors of the past.

The U.S. Constitution and Bill of Rights were formulated not at a whim but long before the first shot was fired. Political theorists and historians such as Thomas Paine whose pamphlet, *Common Sense* influenced almost every American revolutionary.

In the very first paragraph of the pamphlet, Paine makes a distinction which becomes the guiding principle of the new country; namely that society unites people around common causes and that government divides people into separate classes.

"Some writers have so confounded society with government, as to leave little or no distinction between them; whereas they are not only different, but have different origins. Society is produced by our wants, and government by our wickedness; the former promotes our happiness positively by uniting our affections, the latter negatively by restraining our vices. The one encourages intercourse, the other creates distinctions. The first a patron, the last a punisher." – Common Sense

Before this time, most of the world was ruled by monarchies or some form of dictatorship. The government was projected as the "father" and "mother" of the people. The people were considered too ill equipped to govern themselves.

But this time, this new nation would incorporate the concepts of Plato and fellow Greeks. It would pull from Israel, its "judges" to act as a balance to the separation of powers. It would have a "house" for the commoners and a "house" for the "lords" such as developed in England, but this would be the Congress and the Senate. Finally, it would have as the head of state, not a "king" nor even an "esteemed" title but a lowly "presider". A presider was merely a facilitator of a meeting. This presider would become known as the "president"; an office of almost laughable, inglorious counter-prestige. In fact, there were several American "presidents" before the now famous president George Washington. Granted, these other presidents had even less authority than the evolution of the Commander-in-Chief president of today. -- https://en.wikipedia.org/wiki/President_of_the_Contin ental_Congress

The American nation was going to be a "grand experiment" in self-governance. It would attempt to put into action all the principles of those governments and societies tried before.

So, while people may fight over the meaning and intent of the words of the U.S. Constitution and Bill of Rights, its authors were meticulous in their attempt to be clear. Along with those documents are commentary on them called The Federalist Papers. These explicatory documents were written between 1787-1788 by Alexander Hamilton, James Madison, and John Jay. --
https://www.gutenberg.org/cache/epub/18/pg18.html

Hamilton, writing in Essay #9 of the Federalist Papers, specifically had in mind how previous great societies such as the Greeks and Romans could not maintain themselves due to internal strife.

"A FIRM Union will be of the utmost moment to the peace and liberty of the States, as a barrier against domestic faction and insurrection. It is impossible to read the history of the petty republics of Greece and Italy without feeling sensations of horror and disgust at the distractions with which they were continually agitated, and at the rapid succession of revolutions by which they were kept in a state of perpetual vibration

106

between the extremes of tyranny and anarchy. If they exhibit occasional calms, these only serve as short-lived contrast to the furious storms that are to succeed." -- Essay #9

The founders of this new nation wanted to build something more lasting than the societies that litter history. They wanted to learn from the mistakes of those bygone nations, not merely impose their revolutionary Utopia upon the people. They could see that the people were historically prone to squabble and destroy themselves but how could they implement a system that would prevent this repeated "horror and disgust"?

The concept that came out of that question is the paramount of the individual. The USA would not merely be a firm union of states or groups of people but a Republic of the individual whose rights were to be supreme to the state and to factions.

In Essay #10 the idea of the individual versus the faction was expressed:

"By a faction, I understand a number of citizens, whether amounting to a majority or a minority of the whole, who are united and actuated by some common impulse of passion, or of interest, adversed to the rights of other citizens, or to the permanent and aggregate interests of the community.

There are two methods of curing the mischiefs of faction: the one, by removing its causes; the other, by controlling its effects.

There are again two methods of removing the causes of faction: the one, by destroying the liberty which is essential to its existence; the other, by giving to every citizen the same opinions, the same passions, and the same interests.

It could never be more truly said than of the first remedy, that it was worse than the disease. Liberty is to faction what air is to fire, an aliment without which it instantly expires. But it could not be less folly to abolish liberty, which is essential to political life, because it nourishes faction, than it would be to wish the annihilation of air, which is essential to animal life, because it imparts to fire its destructive agency.

The second expedient is as impracticable as the first would be unwise. As long as the reason of man continues fallible, and he is at liberty to exercise it, different opinions will be formed. As long as the connection subsists between his reason and his self-love, his opinions and his passions will have a reciprocal influence on each other; and the former will be objects to which the latter will attach themselves. The diversity in the faculties of men, from which the rights of property originate, is not less an insuperable obstacle to a uniformity of interests. The protection of these faculties is

the first object of government." --
Essay #10
https://en.wikipedia.org/wiki/Federalist_No._10

The protection of the rights of the individual is the "first object of government". Government is not supposed to be perpetuating division and faction by taking from one citizen and giving to another or bestowing on one faction, special rights not afforded to any other citizen. America was supposed to be the truly "classless" society in history where even its highest official was a mere "presider".

If the would-be revolutionary truly seeks to build a Utopia, he or she must glean lessons from societies and governments that have come before. They cannot assume they have come up with the ultimate or thousand-year rule that will withstand all time.

There is a reason the average life cycle of a constitution has historically been about seventeen years, whereas the U.S. Constitution has been in effect for over two-hundred and twenty years. https://www.law.uchicago.edu/news/lifespan-written-constitutions

Add to that, how many other nation's constitutions have been modeled after the U.S. Constitution and Bill of Rights. Unfortunately, some of those attempts have either missed the entire concept of individual rights over the factions or they have left in elements that negate the liberty and protection a constitution is supposed to bring. This is the case with any constitution that enshrines a specific class or religion into the wording, such as many Middle Eastern nations which proclaim Islam as the "official religion" or that "no law can be made that is counter to Islam".

A true constitution does not attempt to enumerate special rights but instead treats all people as individuals and upholds their personhood. There are not different "rights" for male over female or special rights or protections for skin colors or behaviors, such as sexual practices or self-identifications outside the biological facts.

While I'm not saying every successful nation should pattern itself after the USA, a utopian society keeps peace among the factions so that the individual may thrive. For, it is individuals that usually spark revolutions. So, if you anger the wrong individual, you will no doubt be causing the downfall of your own society. Trying to suppress or dismiss this individual will only provoke further determination. You should know, since if you are truly a revolutionary, this is the very thing that caused you to rise up and overthrow your government.

ABOUT THE AUTHOR

RODERICK EDWARDS is the author of books as varied as a fictional account of a person living in a deserted world to an autobiographic about his adoption and reunion, a book about the Universe, to this book about Government overthrow.

Find out more at
amazon.com/author/roderickedwards

Or visit rodericke.com

OTHER BOOKS BY RODERICK

- The Universe: Of Every Religion and None

https://www.amazon.com/dp/1696882419

- Togethermore: Rejection and Reunion

https://www.amazon.com/dp/1688917055

- PVE: A Survivor's Journal

https://www.amazon.com/dp/1980491496

- ONE: Exploration of Individualism

https://www.amazon.com/dp/B01LPBOKO4

- About Preterism: The End is Past

https://www.amazon.com/dp/1079955798

CAN I ASK A FAVOR?

If you enjoyed this book, found it useful or otherwise then I'd really appreciate it if you would post a short review on Amazon. I do read all the reviews personally so that I can continually write what people are wanting.

If you'd like to leave a review then please visit the link below:

amazon.com/author/roderickedwards

Thanks for your support!

INDEX